MAGIC MYST

THE HAUNTED PLAYHOUSE

M

MACMILLAN CHILDREN'S BOOKS

First published in 1985 by Macmillan Children's Books a division of Macmillan Publishers Ltd. London and Basingstoke

ISBN 0 333 38889 5 HB ISBN 0 333 38890 9 PB
Magic Mystery Books are produced by Mushroom Books Ltd. 9 Newburgh Street London W1V 1LH
Origination by Newsele S.R.L. (UK) 01·734 0628 Printed in Italy in association with Keats European Ltd.

Find the clues, solve the mystery and and make a different story every time.

When you read, "Follow the woman to page 34. Or continue your investigations . . . on page 4.", *you* have to decide what to do, then turn to the page you have chosen. It might be ahead, or it might be behind.

Use your skill to make the right choice. If you are hawk-eyed, cunning and sharp-witted, you'll spot the clues, outwit the enemies and uncover the secret. But the *Magic Mystery* doesn't end there. Each story has more than one ending. Some routes lead to success: on some pages you'll catch the villain. Other routes lead to failure: on some pages the villain will catch you! Whatever happens, remember – find the clues, solve the mystery – and make a different story every time.

Solve the mystery of
THE HAUNTED PLAYHOUSE

The Glamis Centre, the new shopping precinct, isn't even completed when the first shopkeepers to move in are moving out again!

"Place is jinxed," says the greengrocer who opens up every morning to a squelched mess of fruit.

"Rotten foundations," says the bookseller whose shelves constantly empty themselves onto the floor.

"Contaminated," says the publican whose beer begins to taste very strange.

"Haunted," says your grandmother – though she won't say why.

You decide to investigate, and you start by attending the official opening ceremony . . . on page 1.

Brandishing a pair of scissors, the Mayor prepares to cut the ribbon. "It gives me great pleasure," he begins.

But the Mayor's big moment is spoiled when someone taps his shoulder. Irritated, he turns round – and stares. He can't believe his eyes!

"It's a ghost!"

"It's a trick!"

"It's a reflection!"

The on-lookers can't believe *their* eyes either. Who or what is it that floats across the square and vanishes through a door? But someone in the crowd is heard to say, "Him again!"

If you want to follow the apparition, go to page 10.☞

Or, if you want to interview the man who recognised it, go to page 21.☞

2

You are a regular customer at the Cloak and Dagger games shop, so the owner allows you to try some new laser disks. You have scored 1,500 points on the 'Haunted House' game when the screen switches to a long, dark corridor. A boy emerges from the shadows and walks towards you. You notice his velvet doublet, lace ruff and short cape.

"Only you can help us," he says. "Come to the Playhouse. Look for me, Robin. Don't fail me."

Then the screen darkens. You rerun the game. There is no corridor, no boy and no sound track. Nothing but cartoon spooks.

If you think that the corridor might be the basement of the Glamis Centre, look for Robin there on page 28. ☞

Or, if you think that the Playhouse must be the old theatre, look there, on page 9. ☞

Duncan seems to know Cawdor Place very well.
"The Duke's Men performed here once," he tells you. "Legend has it that they used to rehearse in that barn."
You enjoy exploring the fascinating old house, but Duncan says, "Let's try the library. I want you to search the local history section while I tackle theatre history."

Agree to help Duncan, and go to the library on page 37. ☞
Or tell him that you want to explore the knot garden. Go there on page 19. ☞

4

You meet the landlord on the doorstep of the Three Sisters pub. "Seen the anti-pest van?" he asks. "We've got rats in the cellar and I want them out by opening time."

He asks you to keep an eye on the pub while he watches from the street corner. You open the cellar flap and listen to the rat-like scurryings and rustlings below. Suddenly, you hear: "Double, double . . ."

"No, no. When the hurlburly's . . . Sit, Grimalkin!"

"Paddock, where art, thou toad! Hover through the fog . . ."

Rats?

Then a cat appears on the ladder. He climbs out and twines around your legs, purring.

"Hello, puss," you say. "Bet you're called 'Spot'."

"I don't care what it's called," growls the landlord, coming through the door. "I hate cats. Out, damned thing!"

Take 'Spot' to the police station on page 11.

Or ask a friend to take him there and continue your investigation at the museum on page 13.

5

The cameras are rolled back into the wings and the theatre falls silent again. Years seem to pass while you wait in the dark. At last there is a sound from the stage. "This is a tale told by an idiot, full of sound and –" A woman dashes out and thrusts a microphone under the speaker's nose. "I'm from T.V. Alpha News," she announces. "I'd like to know why you and your friends are staging this elaborate hoax."

"Away, wench!" says the astonished actor. "Hence, thou trull!"
"Don't you think you're going a little too far?" persists the reporter. "Why not drop the act?"

The exasperated ghost leaps down from the stage – and passes through the floor. "AHHHH!" shrieks the reporter. "He's real! That is, he's not real! That is – Oh no!"

"Got it all on film!" says the cameraman. "We'll broadcast first thing tomorrow! "Your town will be famous!"

The Mayor turns to you. "Don't you dare to stop the haunting!" he hisses. "It's the best tourist attraction we've ever had! This publicity could make the Glamis Centre the next Tower of London!"

6

The students perform *Every Man in his Humour* to an appreciative audience of workmen. They laugh at the jokes, love the disguises and loudly cheer Duncan as the artful Brainworm. But someone doesn't like the play. As the curtain rises on a new act, boos and hisses come from the wings.

Suddenly the curtains fall – literally – engulfing everyone in an ocean of dusty velvet. Up on the balcony, Duncan carries on bravely – until invisible hands push him off, to land in a crumpled heap.

Finally, a deluge of squashy fruit and rotten eggs appears in mid-air and rains down on the stage. Perhaps you chose the wrong play.

Suggest that the students perform another one tomorrow. Try *Macbeth* and go to page 20. ☛
Or try *The Shoemaker's Holiday* and go to page 36. ☛
Or look for more clues about the hauntings. If you haven't been there before, go to the bookshop on page 45. ☛

You race into the shop above, to find the swordsmen still fencing. They seem unaware that their surroundings have changed, but cut and thrust among baths, wash basins and showers. One gains the advantage and traps his opponent against a large tub. It seems that the fight will end – when the trapped man leaps backwards into the tub and lunges at the other's heart! But he loses his balance, slips, and starts the mechanism of a whirlpool jacuzzi!

Suddenly there is a cry of "Enough!" You swing around to see a tall, gaunt woman behind you. The swordsman climbs soddenly from the tub. Both replace their swords in scabbards, bow, and vanish! The woman turns on her heel and strides away, cloak swirling.

Leave the thunder-struck shop assistants gaping.
Follow the woman to page 34. ☞
Or continue your investigations at the Three Sisters pub on page 4. ☞

8

You question the voice in the dark, "Where do you think you are? Who do you think we are?"

"Methinks I be in faery," comes the answer. "Thee be sorcerers!"

"Where have you come from?" you ask.

"I be looking for the barn where we be practising our new play. I gets lost, and I finds myself here, in the dark!"

"Which play?"

"I don't rightly know. Ask our leader. He be lodged not three ells from here, to the East."

"Where? *How* far?"

But there is no answer. The man has gone. You decide to look for the 'leader'. You know which direction is East, but how long is an ell? Try the pharmacy next door, on page 17. ☞
Or go to the pub two doors away, on page 4. ☜
Or try the bookseller on page 45. ☞

The workmen are huddled around a site plan so it's easy to slip past. But instead of leading to a crumbling ruin, the door opens on a page from history.

"Where am I?" you exclaim.

"In the New Playhouse," someone replies.

You spin round. "*When* am I?" you demand.

"In 1598," he tells you. "Let me explain. Time is made of corridors. Sometimes there are holes in the walls between them.

You have just stepped through such a hole."

"Who are you?" you ask. "Why do you speak modern English?"

"I am Dr. Lee," he answers. "They call me a necromancer. You're not the first traveller from the twentieth- century to come here. Duncan taught me your speech. I've asked him to show you around."

If you don't trust Dr. Lee, rush back to your own time and the Glamis Centre. Go to page 23. ☞

Or take the sixteenth-century exit and look for Duncan. Go to page 38. ☞

You run through the door and down some stairs to the basement. Suddenly, an oddly-dressed boy steps through an open door.

"Going to a fancy dress party?" you ask.

"Aiee!" he yelps. "Aroint thee, spirit."

"What do you mean, 'spirit'?" you ask. "I'm real."

The boy touches your sleeve.

"Solid enough," he says, smiling with relief. "My name is Robin. I am bound for Cawdor Place. We practise our play. But I have mislaid my path."

"Up the stairs," you tell him. "Across the precinct. Catch a number twenty-six."

Looking very puzzled, the boy walks on. Follow him to page 18. ☛
Or hurry past him and go upstairs to page 23. ☛

You carry 'Spot', who purrs loudly all the way, to the Police Station. The duty officer notes down his description. "Small, short-haired tom. Grey with black marking on left ear, or was it right?"

He glances down to check.
"Where's he gone?"
"There! On the filing cabinet."
"No, there – on your shoulder."
"On the window ledge!"
"Through the window!"
"Must be a circus cat," says the astonished policeman.
But you saw that 'Spot' wasn't leaping about the station. He was appearing – and disappearing!

Take the same direction as the cat and look for him on page 33.
Or continue your investigations at the delicatessen on page 41.
Or at the pharmacy on page 17.

In the barn three actors are trying to cope with heavy props, a live toad, lighted tapers, a fake fire *and* their lines.

"I be a-weary o' this," complains the first. "And where be thy damned cat?"

"That will be ere set of sun," intones the second, ignoring the first.

The third waves his arms as if casting a spell. Suddenly the cauldron at his feet lifts. The candle flames bend, a great wind howls. You didn't know sixteenth-century special effects were this good!

Crimson smoke boils out of the cauldron. Within a minute you can't see a thing. You hear something lumbering across the floor behind the actors, something heavy, grinding its teeth. Someone throws open the door. The draught reveals three cowled figures dragging tattered robes above thick ankles. They exit pursued by – a shaggy bear!

"– cursed play always brings ill-luck," remarks someone.

You decide it's time you were back in the twentieth-century. If you came through the theatre, go back there on page 27.☞

Or, if you came to the sixteenth-century by another route, ask Duncan how you can return. Go to page 16.☞

You find that the museum is holding a 'fashion through the ages' exhibition. The sixteenth-century section has a tableau of dummies dressed in authentic costumes of rich brocade, intricate embroidery and bright silk.

"Those ruffs must have been uncomfortable," you think aloud.

"Not really," replies the 'sixteenth-century actor', stepping down from the platform. He stretches, yawns, dusts himself off and coolly walks to the door. As soon as his back is turned, the 'sixteenth-century lady' silently rises and glides after him.

Pass the swooning curator and follow the actor to page 29.☞
Or run after the lady to page 34.☞

14

Taking a deep breath, you say, "Robin, I've got something to show you." And you pass him your library book.

"I don't know what half of the words mean," says Robin.

"And I don't believe them. 'Twill never happen."

"It has happened," you tell him gently. "In my time, this is history."

"Then the Duke's men must fly!" he decides. "Thank you!"

You have saved Robin and his friends, but you have also rewritten history. When you return to the twentieth-century, will things have changed? Will you find that the adventure starts again, with events taking a different course? Find out.

Go to page 1.

You dash forward and grab the hem of the man's cloak. But your fingers close on air! Suddenly he jumps,as a spitting furry fury hurls itself at his face.

"Grimalkin!" he exclaims, soothing the angry cat. "Did I step on thy tail?" Then, scooping up the cat, he walks on – straight through the wall!

If you think that man and cat will materialize next door, follow them (using the more ordinary exit) to page 32.☞
Or continue your investigations by interviewing owner of the delicatessen on page 41.☞

16

Back in the great hall, Duncan is singing and playing a lute in the minstrels' gallery. When his song is over, you go up to speak to him.

"You!" he exclaims. "Still here? Look, holes between times don't stay still, you know. They move. The passage which brought you here has closed. You're staying!"
"No!" you insist, aghast. "That's impossible. There must be a way home. How will you go back?"
"I won't," Duncan replies. "I like it here. You will too. You can be my apprentice."
You pick up his lute and study the strings.
"I suppose I can always audition for a part in the next play," you say.

You find no one in the pharmacy but the shop assistant.
Then the door opens a voice booms, "Show yourself!"
"Here, madam," bleats the girl.
"Can I help you?"
"I am Miss Stilcho, the medium.
Kindly turn out the lights."

"But, my customers –" protests the girl.
"Are not important," says Miss Stilcho dismissively.
Suddenly the shelves begin to shake. Bottles and jars rattle all around you.
"The vibrations!" cries Miss Stilcho. "I feel a presence!"
"Yes," snaps a man, coming from the back room. "Me.
Kindly leave my shop."
"But I must hold a seance," wails Miss Stilcho.
"Over my dead body," replies the pharmacist.

As you are shown to the door with Miss Stilcho, you try to explain that you are a serious investigator. But the pharmacist isn't interested. You decide to investigate elsewhere.

If you want to look beneath the Glamis Centre, go down to the basement on page 10. ☚
Or, if you have been down there before, interview the man who recognised the apparition at the opening ceremony. Go to page 21. ☛

18

You follow Robin to the stairs. Instead of climbing, he walks straight through! You have just given directions to a ghost!

As you walk upstairs you hear strange music coming from the precinct. Then you see the musicians.

"Are you ghosts?" you stammer. "No," replies the nearer man. "I'm an advertisement! 'Come to Elizabethan Cawdor Place.' Actually I'm a drama student. This is a vacation job. I'm Duncan."

When you tell Duncan about Robin, he says, "Hmmm. Tell me more over a drink."

"Isn't your friend coming?" you ask.

"What friend?"

You look back at the empty corner – and hurry to catch up with Duncan.

Follow him to the pub garden on page 40.

Or ask him to show you Cawdor Place on page 3.

You explore the colourful garden, half listening to the guide droning away to a party of tourists.

"Here we have the knot garden, so called because flowers were grown here to be picked for 'knots' or posies. Note the small stone beds and geometric lay-out scattered with fragrant herbs."

"What's that?" asks an old lady.

"A rosemary bush."

"And that?"

"A herb called rue."

"And *that?*"

"That's a, that's a – a gh- gh- gh- . . . Ladies and gentlemen, that concludes our tour," stutters the guide, leaving hastily. Suddenly you notice the misty figure drifting along the trellis walk. You hurry after her but by the time you reach the wicket gate, she has gone.

The road leads only to the Glamis Centre, so get on the next bus. If you don't pass her on the way, look for the lady in the car park on page 26.☞

Or race into the shopping precinct on page 34.☞

20

Duncan invites the Mayor, the Town Council and the builders to the play. As the dressing rooms are derelict, the cast change in the foyer and walk to the stage through the auditorium.

"Good luck!" you call to Duncan, who has been out all morning. He ignores you.

"Shh!" whispers the Mayor. "You must say, 'Break a leg'."

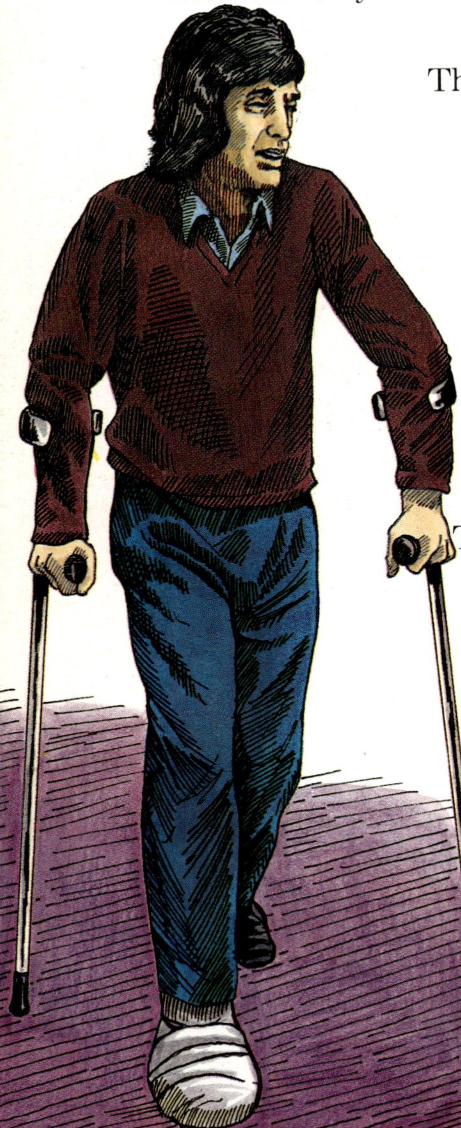

The play is very exciting and Duncan is a very good Macbeth, though he pronounces his lines very oddly. At the end, amid enthusiastic applause, the cast takes a curtain call.

"But where," you ask, "is Duncan?"

"Here!" he puffs, hobbling up the gangway on crutches. "Sorry, everyone. My X-rays took ages. The leg's definitely broken."

Lady Macbeth pales.

"Who was your understudy?" she demands. "I thought it was you."

"What understudy?" asks Duncan. "Surely one of you took over?"

The theatre is searched, but 'Macbeth' is nowhere to be found. After Lady Macbeth recovers from her faint, the Mayor announces that the theatre is saved. Instead of a car park, it is to become a drama workshop.

And the haunting ends.

21

You find the man who seemed to recognise the apparition. "Why did you say 'Him again'?" you ask.

"Because I've seen him before," the man tells you. "I hear him laugh every morning when I unlock my greengrocer's shop and find my best fruit pulped all over the floor! One evening I left my blind up. I came back early and looked through the window. That blighter was hurling my tomatoes at the wall and yelling something about a 'poor player'.

" I rushed in, but he scarpered. Funny, the back door was locked.

"Have any other shop keepers had similar problems?" you ask.

"Oh yes!" replies the greengrocer. "Vandalism's rife! Ask Ms. Lamb at the bookshop, or Birnam, the carpenter."

Talk to the bookseller on page 45.
Or, if you have met her before, talk to the carpenter on page 23.
Or look in at the games shop on page 2.

"Atish-oo!" Robin sneezes loudly.

"Bless you!" you sympathise. "Hayfever? As I was saying –"

Then you notice Robin's white face and shaking hands. He frantically rolls back his sleeve, stares at his arm, then groans miserably.

"What is it?" you ask.

Robin shakes his head.

"Ring a ring o' roses, a pocket full of posies.
Atishoo, atishoo, we all fall down."

"What?"

"I have the plague! Go, quickly, before it claims you!"

You could save Robin. You must rewrite history and warn him and the other actors to leave town before the infection strikes.

Start the adventure again, on page 1.

Walking across the precinct towards the carpenter's store, you see a worried-looking man moaning and tearing his hair. He calls to you, "Have you seen the police? I've 'phoned them, but they think I'm just a crank. Look, will you be a witness? Tell me I'm not insane, please!"

"What's wrong?" you ask.

"It's my stock, my wood. It's moving! It's marching around my workshop!"

You look inside. Sure enough, a procession of planks, logs, sticks and poles is filing up and down.

Suddenly you are elbowed aside. A large, flamboyantly dressed woman sails into the workshop. "What luck!" she booms. "Real psychokinesis! We must hold a seance at once!"

She hands Mr. Birnam a card, saying, "I shall contact the unquiet spirit."

"Can't you just make it go away?" he pleads.

If you want to watch Miss Stilcho's seance, go to page 39. ☞

Or, if you don't think that the workshop is haunted at all, go to the games shop. Go to page 2. ☚

"You're a fake!" you accuse Miss Stilcho. "I've seen T.V. programmes about people like you!" You replace the table and roll up the blind.

"How did you answer yourself?" you ask. "Ventriloquism?"

Then you notice someone sitting in the corner, blinking in the sunlight.

Suddenly he leaps to his feet, crying,

"Where be I? This place be haunted!"

Everyone is frozen to the spot. Before anyone recovers, the man rushes through the door and across the square. You hurry after him in time to see him disappear into a narrow passage.

The passage leads to only two places: the wine bar and the burger bar. If you want to search the wine bar, go to page 30. ☞

Or, if you have already visited the wine bar, look in the burger bar. Go to page 29. ☞

Duncan shows you around the old theatre and tells you its history. "This building was erected after the old playhouse burned down," he says. "If the plague hadn't wiped them out, the Duke's Men would have performed here on Midsummer's Day, 1598. It's the anniversary tomorrow."

"Tomorrow, and tomorrow and tomorrow . . ." comes an eerie murmur from the stage. Duncan starts, grabs your arm and pulls you after him. You can just make out a man amid the dust and gloom.

He is pacing the stage, declaiming and making grand, sweeping gestures. He stamps his foot, complaining, "Zounds! 'Twill not come right."

Duncan points at the boards of the stage. The man's feet are beneath them! "He's walking on the level of the old playhouse," he whispers.

"Forsooth," mutters the actor, " 'Tis a part hard to con."

"It's Will Cant!" exclaims Duncan. Startled, the ghost looks up, and vanishes.

"I knew it!" Duncan cries. "The Duke's Men are still rehearsing, after four centuries! Come on!"

Duncan leads you to page 46. ☞

26

Near the car park you see a throng of people, faces upturned. You follow their gaze to a tall figure gliding across the roof. Her arms are outstretched, like a sleepwalker's, and she is wringing her hands.

You race inside and jab the lift button. The second the doors open at the roof you dash out and run to the balustrade. The woman is still there, pacing and – waving to the crowd! "Come to the Poly Theatre tonight and tomorrow!" she calls. "Don't miss the Rag Week Review: Shakespeare on skateboards!"

As she glides past you to the lift,you hear the scrunch of wheels under her gown.

"Are you the only student advertising the review?" you ask.

"Oh no," she replies. "Lots of us are staging stunts like this."

You've heard enough. You follow her to the lift, and make for home.

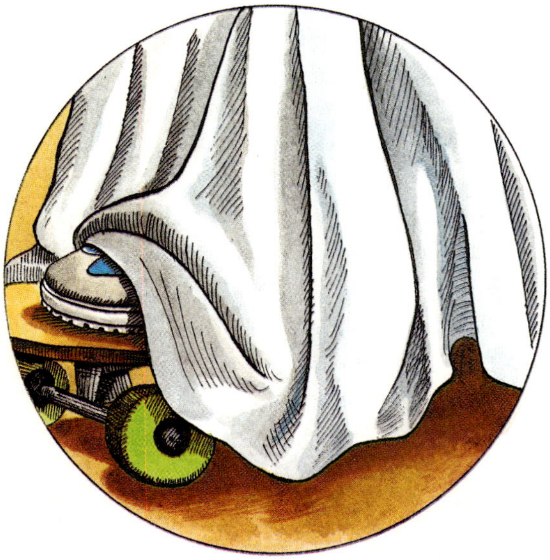

You step through the doorway, wondering whether anyone will see you arrive in the twentieth-century, and how you will explain your mysterious appearance. But you needn't have worried, because you step out on the other side, still in 1598! Someone taps your arm. "Did'st note my part?" he asks shyly.

"Was't good? Will said, 'Robin doth promise fairly'. Dost agree?" Then he notices your air of gloom and asks, "What ails thee?" You tell him. "Mayhap you have tarried over long," he suggests. "Consult Duncan, the minstrel."

If you went to the library before you came to the sixteenth-century, take the book you borrowed and go to page 14. ☛
Or, if you haven't been to the library, talk to Duncan on page 16. ☛

You walk the silent corridors below the centre until raised voices, coming from an empty office, stop you in your tracks. You put your head around the door, and see a sword fight!

"Again!" says the first swordsman. "Lunge, parry, cut, sidestep. My cape. So! Stumble and – so!" And he thrusts his sword into his opponent's chest!

Horrified, you open your mouth to scream, "Murder!" but the swordsman withdraws his rapier, and bends it in half! "Methinks yon false blade will fool no one," he complains.
" 'Tis real enough," reassures the other. "I have it now. Again."

The pair progress along the corridor, fencing with gusto. You follow them but, to your amazement, they mount an invisible staircase and, still fighting, disappear into the ceiling!

Find some stairs which you can see and go to the shop above your head on page 7.
Or decide that you've been dreaming and go on to the theatre on page 9.

You go through the huge glass doors of the burger bar and walk up to the long chrome counter.

"You haven't by any chance seen a funny-looking chap in doublet and hose, have you?" you ask the chef. To your amazement, he leans across and throws his arms around you, saying, "Thank you! Thank you!"

You explain about your investigations. The chef nods happily.

"So I'm not having delusions!" he says. "Or you're having the same ones. I've seen that man sitting at table ten. But whenever I say, 'This is self-service', (or something like that) he vanishes! Who is he?"

You explain, then wonder what to do next.

If you have worked out the secret of the haunted playhouse, go to the Mayor's parlour and explain it to him. Go to page 44. ☞

Or, if you don't yet know how to stop the haunting, investigate the theatre. Go to page 33. ☞

The wine bar is closed. You knock and call loudly, but there is no reply. The door is unlocked, so you go inside. The owner is obviously decorating the place for another of his 'Elizabethan banquets'. It doesn't feel like morning at all in here. It's dark, silent and rather eerie. You walk between rough trestle tables laden with wooden trenchers, calling, "Anyone about?" No one answers, but a movement at the high table attracts your attention. The flickering light passes through the doublet of the man sitting there. You gape at him, your jaw dropping. He spots you, starts, and gets up. Then he walks straight for the wall.

Leap forward and grab his cloak before he can get away.
Go to page 15.
Or let him walk through the wall, then look for him in the shop next door. Go to page 32.

Duncan leads you to Cawdor Place. "You can take a quick look round," he says. "But then you must go. Don't worry, no one will notice you. The Duke has invited the whole town to his wedding banquet."

Duncan joins the other musicians strolling through the crowd. You sample the strange food and watch the antics of the Duke's jester. You are enjoying yourself. Why should you obey Duncan and hurry home?

If you think that he must have had a good reason to warn you like that, go home and start again on page 1.

Or, if you think that he's just cross because you've found your way here too, explore Cawdor Place for an hour or so and then find Duncan on page 16.

Or look in on the rehearsal in the barn on page 12.

32

You run into the next shop and squeeze past shelves of masks, boxes of props and racks and racks of brightly coloured costumes. It's an eerie place, with something to make you jump in every corner. Suddenly the light goes out! You try to feel your way to the door. It opens in front of you and reveals – a skeleton! You reel back in terror, then throw yourself forward again as you stumble against something tall and furry.

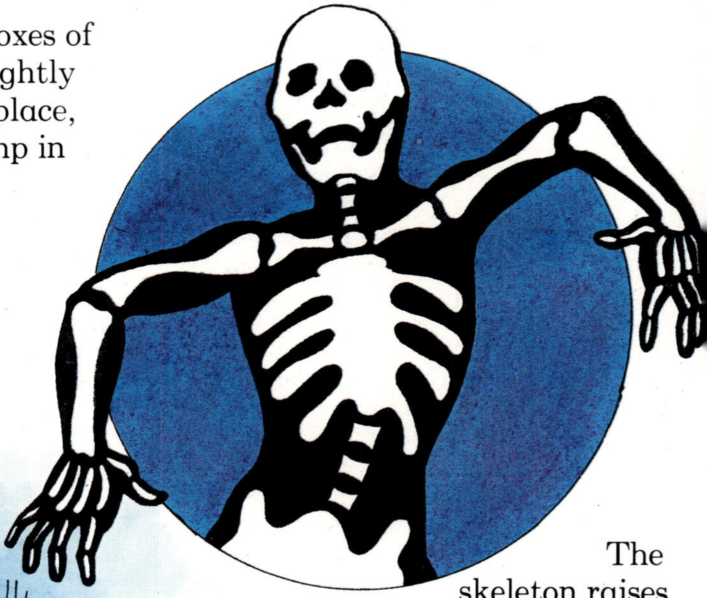

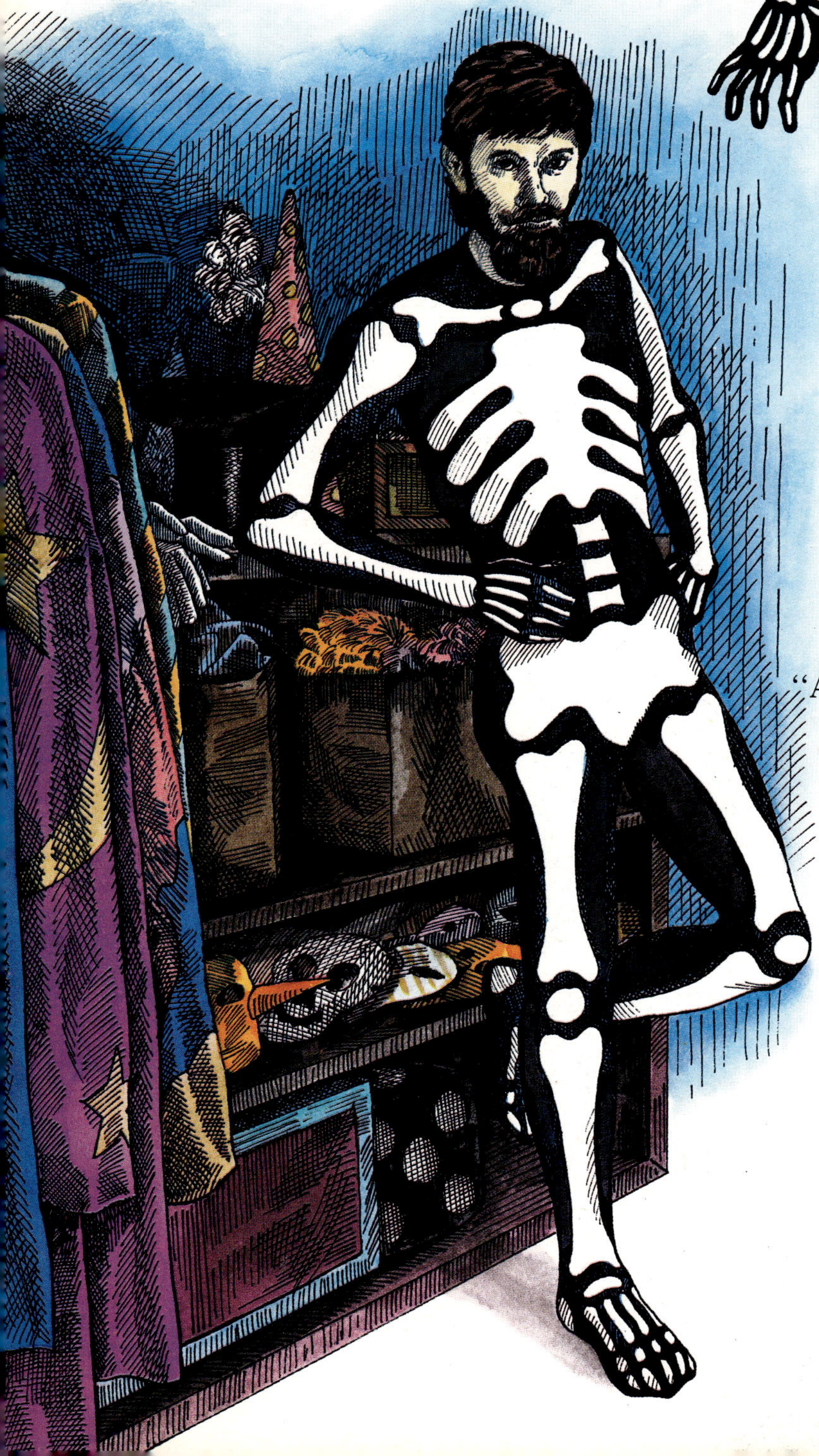

The skeleton raises a boney hand and rips off its skull, which grins at you from under its arm. You cower in fear, covering your eyes with your hands. The light comes on.

"It's O.K., it's only me," says a reassuringly human voice. You open your fingers a crack and see the shopkeeper, dressed in a luminous skeleton costume.

"Sorry!" he says. "I'm getting my own back on some practical jokers who've been breaking in here and trying to scare me."

"Are you sure they're jokers?" you ask.

"Oh yes. What else? Someone has broken into a lot of shops recently. You ask at the bookshop, or the delicatessen."

Go to the bookshop on page 45. ☛
Or, if you've already been there, go to the delicatessen on page 41. ☛

33

As you arrive, a big crane is hoisting a huge lead ball, ready to smash the old theatre to rubble. Standing by the crane is the site foreman, arguing loudly with a man who shouts, "You're destroying centuries of history! Under this Victorian building are Elizabethan cellars, mediaeval foundations! It needs careful excavation, years of sifting, sorting –"

"It's having a car park," says the foreman firmly. "Swing away, lads!"

All eyes turn to the lead ball – and stare at it – transfixed. Poised, one hand on the chain, stands a tall, strangely dressed man holding a lethal-looking rapier.

"Varlets!" he calls. "Groundlings! Approach at your peril!"

Suddenly he disappears – and materializes on the cabin roof of the crane. "Fight like a man!" he challenges the retreating driver. Every workman in sight edges away, ready to run.

The theatre is safe for a while. If you want to try to preserve it forever, ask the Mayor's help.

Go to page 44.

34

Looking up, you see the lady in the distance. But, though you run until you think your lungs will burst, you can't catch her. Yet she doesn't seem to be hurrying. Heart pounding, head down, you sprint across the precinct. You notice moss in the cracks between the paving slabs, then grass pushing through cracks in the concrete. The Glamis Centre is getting tatty already. You glance ahead. Despite your best effort, the lady is still just as far ahead. Suddenly you realise that the going is softer.

You are running on turf. You stop. Where on earth are you? No exit from the shopping precinct leads to open country like this. And where's the lady? There's no sign of her.

If you want to continue in the same direction, go to page 43. ☞
Or turn back and make for the buildings on the horizon. Go to page 38. ☞

You go down to the basement again and find the spot where you met Robin. For a long time nothing happens, then you hear a boy laughing, and Robin comes running through the wall.

"I wish you wouldn't do that!" you exclaim. "It makes me jump."

"But you're not afraid of me now?" he asks.

"No!" you say.

"Good! Dr. Lee has told me that you are no spirit – and nor am I!"

You notice that Robin is wearing different clothes. More time has passed for him than for you.

"How's the play?" you ask.

"It goes well," Robin tells you. "Poor Tom fell sick, but we have another porter."

If you have been to the library, Robin's comment will remind you to show him the book you borrowed. Go to page 14.

Or, if you haven't been to the library, go on talking to Robin. Go to page 22.

Half way through the first act of *The Shoemaker's Holiday,* several people walk up the aisle to the front row.

"I'm afraid you'll have to bring down the curtain," says a police sergeant. "The town bailiff here has orders to demolish this place. You are obstructing these gentlemen."

The builders' foreman grins as, clutching their makeshift props and scripts, the actors jump down from the stage.

"Pity," remarks Duncan. "We'll never know if that would have cured the haunting."

Then one of the builders whispers, "You can still hold the play. We won't start 'till tomorrow lunchtime."

"Right," says Duncan. "We'll come back tomorrow."

If you want to try a different play, suggest *Every Man in his Humour*. Go to page 6.

Or try *Macbeth*. Go to page 20.

Or abandon the idea of staging a play. Come back to watch the demolition on page 33.

37

The library has a large local history section and you soon find a book about the old theatre. You borrow it and immediately begin to read.

You learn that a troupe of strolling players called the Duke's Men came to town in 1598. After entertaining the guests at the Duke's wedding, they

settled down to rehearse a new play in one of his barns. When one of the company became ill, they hired a newcomer to take his place. But the stranger had the plague! One by one the other actors caught the disease. There were no survivors.

Taking the book with you, go to the old theatre on page 33.

Or, if you'd like to learn more about the sixteenth-century, go to the museum on page 13.

38

You walk along a cobbled street, past gabled houses which lean at improbable angles. Wrinkling your nose at the terrible stench of the open gutter, you identify fish among the smells. Just ahead you see knots of people rummaging in, bartering for and gossiping around large baskets of herring.
"A sixteenth-century Glamis Centre," you think.
"Idiot! Watch out!" someone shouts, thrusting you aside. The contents of a slop bucket, emptied from an upper window, land at your feet.

"Thanks!" you say. "But your Elizabethan English is slipping!"
"Oops! Prithee, woulds't care to follow your servant, Duncan the Minstrel to Cawdor Place?"

If you would like to see a Tudor Mansion, go with Duncan to page 31.
Or, if you would like to see the Duke's Men in the flesh, ask Duncan the way to the barn where they are rehearsing. Go to page 12.

Miss Stilcho rolls down the blind and sits at a table, arms outstretched.
"Unquiet spirit!" she calls. "Whoever you are, speak! If you have a message for us, knock once. If not, knock twice."
The table lifts onto two legs, then falls with a thud.
You watch Miss Stilcho carefully.
"Are you from the theatre?" she asks.
THUD
"Are you one of the Duke's Men?"
THUD
"Can you speak to us?"
"I do prate as fine as thee, Beldame!"

If you don't believe that Miss Stilcho has really contacted a spirit, go to page 24. ☛

Or, if you do believe that Miss Stilcho is a medium, go to page 8. ☛

40

Once you are settled with a lemonade in the garden of the Three Sisters pub, you tell Duncan the rest of your story.

"That fits my theory," he tells you. "I was at the opening ceremony. I saw the chap who nearly scared Mayor Graham to death. He looked exactly like a portrait I've seen of Will Cant, the famous actor." Suddenly the barmaid runs into the garden. "That's it!" she shouts, tearing off her apron. "I resign! Grey ladies in the bar I can stand. Headless horsemen in the car park are old hat. But when the pumps refuse to pull up anything but *mead* – it's just too much!"

Ignoring the interruption, Duncan continues, "I believe that the Glamis Centre is haunted by sixteenth-century actors. For some reason they don't want to leave the old theatre. But why?"

Duncan asks you to investigate the old theatre with him.
Agree and go to page 25.
Or, if you think that Robin might be involved in Duncan's theory, look for him again in the basement of the Glamis Centre. Go to page 35.

The delicatessen is locked but when you hammer on the window the owner appears, mouthing, "Sorry, closed".
You shout, "I want to talk!" and he unlocks the door.

"It's about the haunting," you begin.
"You too?" he cries. "Look at these!"
He pulls you inside and points to a photographic developing tray.

"I loaded an automatic camera with superfast film last night," he tells you. "It took these pictures between midnight and two a.m."
"Good grief!" you exclaim.
"A phantom midnight feast!"
The delicatessen owner is hurling things into a case.
"They ate every morsel of my roast goose, pheasants, grouse, cheese, bread – but they didn't open a single tin, and they didn't go near the freezer. This place is nothing but a larder for a troupe of spooks. I'm off, and I'm not the only one. Go to the bookshop, or the pharmacy, you'll see!"

If you want to talk to Ms. Lamb at the bookshop, go to page 45.
Or, if you want to interview Mr. Jones, the pharmacist, go to page 17.

42

You begin your vigil in the wings of the old theatre, slowly growing very stiff, very cold, and just a little frightened. You have the eeriest feeling that something is lurking among the shadowy flats at the back of the stage.

Faintly, the town hall clock strikes midnight. Suddenly a shaft of light illuminates a solitary figure. It follows him as he paces up and down, slapping his forehead, as if trying to remember something. Then he snaps his fingers and briskly steps to the front of the stage. As he walks, his ghostly spotlight dims, and darkness swallows him.

A far brighter light dazzles you. People swarm from the back of the stage, hauling lights, microphones, cameras, and all talking at once.

"What's happening?" you ask the nearest person.

"We're from T.V. Alpha," she tells you. "We're covering the so-called 'hauntings'."

"You'll frighten them away," you protest. "They'll never hold their first night."

"What?" she asks scornfully. "Don't tell me you believe that stuff. It's a great story, but . . ."

Promise to be quiet and you'll be allowed to watch on page 5. ☛

You walk on for about ten minutes without seeing a soul.

Then someone calls, "Hail!".
You lean over a hedge and see three of the strangest creatures imaginable squatting around a big iron bowl.
"Hail, Thane of Glamis!" says one.
"Glamis!" you exclaim. "Can you direct me to the Centre, please?"
"What, knave?" growls the second.
"Durst mar our scene? Begone!"
"Sorry, don't understand," you say.
The message is about to be made clear with a large ladle when the weird trio begin to fade. Slowly they become transparent – and in their place appears – the Glamis Centre.

Brandishing a pair of scissors, the Mayor prepares to cut the ribbon. You're back at the opening ceremony! Did you dream today? Are you under a spell? Or have you stumbled on a loop in time?

Find out. Start the adventure again on page 1.

You hurry to the Mayor's parlour and blurt out your story. At first he won't listen.

"That incident at the ceremony was unfortunate," he says. "Gossip and silly stories have been circulating ever since. It was a trick of the light. They do it with mirrors, you know."

Sadly, you leave. But no sooner have you closed the door than you hear the Mayor calling you. You go back inside to find the Mayor sitting at his desk – a metre in the air!

"Get me down!" he begs. "I believe your story. Let's lay these phantoms to rest. What do I have to do?"

If you think that Duncan will know what to do, ask him. Go to page 20.

Or persuade the Mayor to join you at the theatre for some midnight ghost-spotting. Go to page 42.

You find Ms. Lamb scrambling about in a chaotic mess of books, papers, magazines and broken shelves, muttering, "I can't stand it! I'm leaving! *Architects!*"

As you enter the shop, she snaps, "We're closed! I can't possibly find a book to sell you from *this.*"

But when you explain about your investigations, she drops the paperbacks she is sorting, sits back on her heels and says severely, "Nothing mysterious about this. It's shaky foundations. Every time a fast train passes nearby, my entire stock plummets to the floor. Builders!"

Ms. Lamb picks up her books again, dismissing you, but as you turn to go she calls, "Try the wine bar. The owner's a nervous type. No doubt he'll have some weird and wonderful tales for you. If you hurry, you'll catch him before he opens."

Visit the wine bar on page 30.
Or, if you have been to the wine bar before, try the library. Go to page 37.

Duncan introduces you to his drama student friends. He explains his theory about the hauntings to them, saying, "In my opinion, the Duke's Men are still trying to perform their play. I think we should give them a first night."

"Yes!" cries a girl student eagerly. "We can use scripts and stage the play at once. Which play is it?"

"That's the snag," admits Duncan ruefully. "No one knows which play the Duke's Men planned to perform. I've done some research and I think it was either *The Shoemaker's Holiday,* or *Macbeth* or *Every Man in his Humour.*"

He turns to you.

"As our official ghost spotter," he says, "you can choose."

If you think that the Duke's Men were rehearsing *The Shoemaker's Holiday,* go to page 36.

Or, if you think that it was *Macbeth,* go to page 20.

Or, if you think it was *Every Man in his Humour,* go to page 6.